WE THE PEOPLE

Angel Island

by Alice K. Flanagan

Content Adviser: Amy Sueyoshi, Ph.D.,
Assistant Professor, Ethnic Studies Program,
San Francisco State University

Reading Adviser: Rosemary G. Palmer, Ph.D.,
Department of Literacy, College of Education,
Boise State University

COMPASS POINT BOOKS

MINNEAPOLIS, MINNESOTA

Compass Point Books
3109 West 50th Street, #115
Minneapolis, MN 55410

Visit Compass Point Books on the Internet at *www.compasspointbooks.com*
or e-mail your request to *custserv@compasspointbooks.com*

On the cover: Group portrait of Chinese women, Angel Island, c. 1925

Photographs ©: Courtesy of State Museum Resource Center, California State Parks, cover, 4, 11, 15, 27, 30; Prints Old & Rare, back cover (far left); Library of Congress, back cover, 24; Mary Evans Picture Library, 6; Owen Franken/Corbis, 7; The Bancroft Library, University of California, Berkeley, 8, 26, 31, 33; San Francisco History Center, San Francisco Public Library, 10, 35, 36; Hulton Archive/Getty Images, 13; North Wind Picture Archives, 16, 17, 18, 19; The Granger Collection, New York, 21, 23, 28; AP Photo/Jacub Mosur, 32; Philip Gould/Corbis, 38; Catherine Karnow/Corbis, 39; John Elk III, 40; Bettmann/Corbis, 41.

Editor: Jennifer VanVoorst
Designer/Page Production: Bradfordesign, Inc./The Design Lab
Photo Researcher: Svetlana Zhurkin
Cartographer: XNR Productions, Inc.
Educational Consultant: Diane Smolinski
Library Consultant: Kathleen Baxter

Managing Editor: Catherine Neitge
Creative Director: Keith Griffin
Editorial Director: Carol Jones

Library of Congress Cataloging-in-Publication Data
Flanagan, Alice K.
  Angel Island / by Alice K. Flanagan.
    p. cm. — (We the people)
  Includes bibliographical references and index.
  ISBN 0-7565-1261-1 (hardcover)
  1. Angel Island (Calif.)—History—20th century—Juvenile literature. 2. Chinese Americans—History—20th century—Juvenile literature. 3. United States—Emigration and immigration—History—20th century—Juvenile literature. 4. China—Emigration and immigration—History—20th century—Juvenile literature.
I. Title. II. Series: We the people (Series) (Compass Point Books)
  F868.S156F59 2006
  979.4'62—dc22   2005002460

TABLE OF CONTENTS

THE JOURNEY TO AMERICA

One gray morning in 1934, two Chinese teenagers stepped off a steamship docked in San Francisco Bay harbor, California. They felt the solid ground beneath their feet and breathed a sigh of relief that their long 7,000-mile (11,200-kilometer) journey across the Pacific Ocean was finally over. These two young men were immigrants. They had left behind their homeland and come to live in the United States.

Immigrants arrived at Angel Island after a long sea journey.

Sixteen-year-old Lee Kim Wong was the son of a poor farmer. For generations his family had struggled to farm a small piece of land near the Pearl River in Canton, China. It was a difficult place to grow food. When he was unable to earn enough money to help support his family, he came to America to find work. He was going to help support his family in China with the money he earned.

Seventeen-year-old Ieoh Ming Pei was the son of a successful banker. His family was well known in Canton's business community. Ieoh was interested in how buildings were designed and wanted to become an architect. Because Ieoh thought he would get a better education in America, his father sent him there to study.

Lee and Ieoh had different backgrounds and very different reasons for coming to America. Both were following their dreams, but only Ieoh would see his dreams come true. At the time, the United States had a limit, called a quota, on the number of Chinese immigrants it allowed into the country. Americans did not want Chinese

A cartoon from the 1880s shows Uncle Sam waving back a boat of Chinese immigrants.

workers, like Lee Kim Wong, to come and take jobs away from them.

Ieoh was a student and the son of a banker, so he was excused from the rules that kept people like Lee Kim

Wong from entering the United States. After Ieoh Ming Pei came to the United States, he studied architecture and eventually became a famous architect. Some of his best-known buildings are the entrance to the Louvre Museum in Paris, France, and the John F. Kennedy Library in Boston, Massachusetts.

Because Lee Kim Wong was coming to find common work, he was sent to Angel Island Immigration Station, where he was questioned about his family. After

Chinese immigrant I.M. Pei designed this entrance to the Louvre Museum.

7

Angel Island Immigration Station was the first stop for many immigrants.

being held there for several weeks, Lee was sent back to China. Thousands of other Chinese immigrants in the 1900s shared a similar experience. Why were they detained at Angel Island? More importantly, why were immigration officials keeping them out of the United States?

THE HISTORY OF ANGEL ISLAND

Angel Island is one of the largest islands in California's San Francisco Bay. In 1775, the Spanish explorer Don Juan Manuel Ayala sailed into the bay, stopping at what is now

Angel Island is one of several islands in San Francisco Bay.

Ayala Cove. His men explored the bay and made a map of the region. Because the island seemed to protect the bay like a guardian angel, Ayala named it "Isla de Los Angeles"—Spanish for Island of the Angels.

In 1910 the United States built an immigration station at the northeast corner of the island in the area known as China Cove. For the next 30 years it served as the main point of entry for thousands of immigrants coming into the United States through the West Coast. It was known

Angel Island Immigration Station was a complex of many buildings.

Few European immigrants entered the United States through Angel Island.

as the "Guardian of the Western Gate."

The immigration station was set up to receive people from Asia and Europe. However, only a few Europeans were ever detained at Angel Island during these years. Japanese immigrants, too, were generally allowed to enter San Francisco soon after their ship docked and their paperwork was sent to the immigration station. For the most part, immigration officials detained only the Chinese whom they wanted to keep out of the United States.

WHY THE CHINESE CAME

The Chinese began coming to the United States in the 1840s, shortly after gold was discovered in California. At the time, wars and poverty in China forced many young men to leave their homeland for a better life. Believing the stories they had heard about streets "paved with gold," the Chinese joined more than a half-million other people from around the world who flooded into the California mountains searching for gold. The Chinese called California "Gam Saan"—Land of the Golden Mountains. Newspapers called this worldwide event the "Gold Rush."

Like all hopeful miners, the Chinese believed that they would get rich quickly in California. Then they would return home to take a place of honor in their families. But discrimination kept the Chinese from mining in areas where gold was plentiful, and taxes took money away from those who did well. Only a few lucky individuals ever made a fortune as miners. Usually, the Chinese worked together and shared what they found. Whenever they could, they sent money home to their families.

Many Chinese left their homeland to look for gold in California.

One young man described why his father left China and traveled to the United States. He said, "We were very, very much in debt because of the local warfare. We planted each year, but we were robbed. We had to borrow. When news about the gold rush in California was spread by the shippers, my father decided to take a big chance."

In those days, most Chinese peasants were making only about $20 a year. Because a ticket to America cost around $50, many people had to borrow money from family members or neighbors. Some sold their houses and even their land to buy a ticket. Others got money from merchants. If a merchant agreed to pay for a ticket, however, an immigrant had to work a set number of years for the merchant until the money was paid back.

In the early days, immigrants traveled to America on sailing ships. Because these ships depended on the power of the wind to move them, it could take anywhere from 50 to 100 days to get to America. One immigrant described his experience aboard ship in a letter to his family. He wrote, "When the wind was good and strong, we made much headway. But for days there would be no wind … and the ship would drift idly on the smooth sea." As a rule, sailing from China to the United States took about two months. When steamships replaced sailing ships, the trip took only a few weeks.

Steamships like this one dramatically reduced travel time to the United States.

15

Conditions aboard ships in the 1800s were generally unpleasant. Food and water were usually in short supply. As one immigrant remembered: "Not a drop [of water] was allowed to be wasted for washing our faces; and so, when rain came, we eagerly caught the rainwater and did our washing." And because many Chinese immigrants were poor, they were put in the steerage, the least expensive section of the ship. The steerage was overcrowded. Sometimes immigrants had to take turns sleeping in the same bed. Because of the crowded conditions, illness

16

The steerage section of the ship was crowded and unsanitary.

spread quickly among the immigrants. Many of them died before ever reaching America.

In 1851, a second wave of Chinese laborers started to arrive in the United States. This group of immigrants came to California to build the western half of the transcontinental railroad, and they continued to arrive through 1864.

Chinese laborers helped build all of the railroads in the western United States.

17

After the railroad was completed in 1869, many
Chinese took various jobs on farms and ranches. Using
their knowledge of farming, these immigrants created
successful fruit-growing businesses and helped build the
first vineyards in California.

Other Chinese immigrants worked to improve the
fishing and canning businesses along the West Coast from

Some Chinese railroad laborers later worked in California vineyards.

Stores in San Francisco's Chinatown catered to the tastes of Chinese immigrants.

San Diego north to Alaska. Those who settled in the San Francisco Bay area opened grocery stores, restaurants, and laundry shops. The neighborhood where their businesses were located was called "Chinatown."

19

CHINESE ARE NOT WELCOME!

More than 300,000 Chinese laborers entered the United States between 1849 and 1882. In those days, there were no immigration laws, such as quotas, to keep people out of the country. Everyone came and went freely. This freedom was due in part to the Burlingame Treaty, an agreement that the United States and China signed in 1868. It gave American and Chinese citizens the freedom to travel back and forth between the United States and China and stay as long as they liked. The treaty was named after Anson Burlingame, an American official serving in China at that time.

When the Chinese first began to settle in the United States, they were welcomed—especially by business owners. The Chinese took jobs that no one else wanted, and they were willing to work long hours for low wages. But when companies began hiring Chinese workers for jobs that

20

Americans wanted, feelings toward the Chinese changed. Some angry American workers attacked the Chinese, believing that the Chinese were taking away their jobs. In remembering these times, one Chinese man said, "We kept indoors after dark for fear of being shot in the back. Children spit upon us as we passed by and called us rats."

As the persecution got worse, mobs destroyed Chinese homes and businesses, killing women and children in the process. Afraid for their lives, many Chinese

In 1885, 15 Chinese coal miners in Wyoming were killed by a mob of white miners.

21

fled east to larger towns. When riots began breaking out in several cities, the U.S. government passed laws to stop more Chinese from coming to the United States.

The laws, which were passed in 1882, were called Exclusion Laws. They kept Chinese laborers out of the United States for 10 years. They did not, however, exclude Chinese teachers, tourists, merchants, students, or their wives and children. These people were allowed to live and work in the United States even though they could not become citizens. When their children were born in the United States, however, they became citizens at birth.

Later on, other laws were passed to limit a Chinese person's right to travel. One of these laws said that "no Chinese laborer in the United States shall be permitted, after having left, to return hereto." Only individuals whose wives or children lived in the United States were allowed to leave and return. Those who owned land or businesses worth more than $1,000 could leave and return also.

Another law made all Chinese laborers in the United

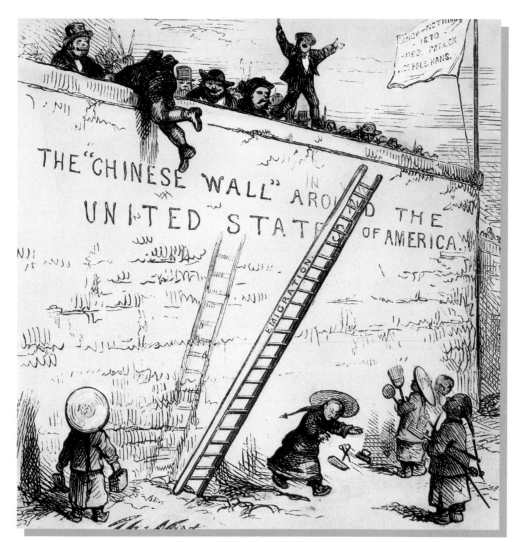

The U.S. government passed laws to prevent Chinese from entering the country.

States carry papers to prove that they lived in the United States. Anyone found without a paper could be arrested and returned to China.

PROVING CITIZENSHIP

The Exclusion Laws continued to limit the number of Chinese entering and leaving the United States through the 1940s. However, in 1906, an earthquake and fire destroyed parts of San Francisco, including the Hall of Records. This building held all the city's marriage, birth, and death certificates. After these papers were gone, many

Much of San Francisco was destroyed in the 1906 earthquake and fire.

Chinese people began claiming that they had been born in the United States and were citizens. As citizens, they could travel freely and bring their families from China.

Since it was now impossible to check if citizenship claims were true, U.S. authorities had to give the Chinese the papers that would allow their family members to come to the United States. Many Chinese used this situation to their advantage. When they were asked to name their family members, they included extra ones who did not exist. The Chinese sold these extra family member names to other immigrants who were waiting to bring their relatives into the United States. Those who pretended to be children of American citizens were known as "paper sons" and "paper daughters." They were not really related. Their connection to the families existed only on paper.

The cost to become a paper son or daughter was about $100 per year of age. This amount bought the papers needed to come to the United States, but it still did not ensure that the person would be allowed to enter. He or

25

In the matter of the
identification of
PON DOO CHEW,
merchant's minor son.
Student and traveler
for curiosity and
pleasure.

Prior landing :- No. 14517/12-16,
ex ss "Manchuria" July 20,1915.

State of California)
City and County of)ss
San Francisco   )

Photograph of
PON DOO CHEW

      Pon Doo Chew, being first duly sworn upon oath,
according to law, doth depose and say :-

      That affiant is a resident Chinese person, lawfully
domiciled within the United States, having arrived at the Port
of San Francisco, on the ss "Manchuria", on the 20th day of July,
1915, No. 14517/12-16, and after due a nd proper investigation
affiant was permitted to enter the United States, your affiant
being the minor son of a resident Chinese merchant lawfully
domiciled therein.

      That your affiant's father is Pon Hing, a resident
Chinese merchant lawfully domiciled within the United States.
That the said Pon Hing is now , and has been for more than a
year prior to the date hereof, a merchant and member of the firm
of Mow Lee and Co., which is a firm engaged in buying and
selling merchandise at a fixed place of business, to wit:- at No.
720 Grant Avenue, San Francisco, during which time he has engaged
in the performance of no manual labor except such as was necessary
in the conduct of his business, and that your affiant has lived
with his said father since his entry into the United States,
as aforesaid.

      That shortly after the landing of your affiant
in the United States he became a student in the Oriental
Public School, at San Francisco, where he remained a student
until just prior to the present time, when he was making
arrangements to go to China upon a temporary visit as
a traveler for curiosity and pleasure, and to visit his
mother and relatives in China, and that this affidavit is
made to facilitate in establishing the identity of your
affiant as such merchant's minor son, student and traveler
for curiosity and pleasure.

Chinese immigrants could buy papers that gave them
a legal identity in the United States.

she had to prove family ties by correctly answering

very specific questions that Angel Island immigration

authorities asked them.

KEEPING THE CHINESE OUT

As soon as immigrants arrived at Angel Island Immigration Station, they were separated into three groups: Whites, Japanese and other Asians, and Chinese. Then the men and women were also separated. Children under the age of 12 stayed with their mothers.

The immigrants were taken to the island hospital for a health exam. Because many of the Chinese immigrants had come from areas where health conditions were poor,

Many of the Japanese women who came to the United States did so as mail-order brides.

27

U.S. officials examined them more carefully than others. If they had diseases that could spread, they were kept from entering the country.

Those who passed the health exam then waited for

28

Only Chinese who passed the health exam were allowed to enter the United States.

their papers to be examined. U.S. authorities were looking for paper sons and daughters among the Chinese. The authorities believed that most Chinese lied to gain entry into the United States and were not related to U.S. citizens at all. To keep the "paper families" out, authorities asked these immigrants questions that they thought only real family members would know.

To prepare for these questions, immigrants studied information about their pretend families from "coaching papers" or "coaching letters." They purchased these papers along with false identity papers before leaving China and memorized the information during the long ocean trip. Then before the ship arrived in San Francisco Bay, they destroyed the papers or tossed them overboard.

Sometimes, immigrants received coaching information while they were detained at Angel Island. Chinese families in San Francisco paid the kitchen staff at the immigration station to carry information to the immigrants. A gardener or a night watchman on the island

This coaching message was hidden inside an orange.

might also supply information. Often, they hid the papers in clothing or food. Once, a piece of paper was even put in a peanut shell.

Usually, immigration officials began the questioning by asking the immigrants to describe their parents, grandparents, and other family members. Next, they asked them very specific questions about their home in China such as, "How far is your village from the bamboo tree? How many steps are there to the front door of your house? Where did your family keep its rice?" Then, their relatives in the United States were asked the same questions to see if their answers matched. This was a difficult test, even for real relatives. For many of these people, it had been 20 years

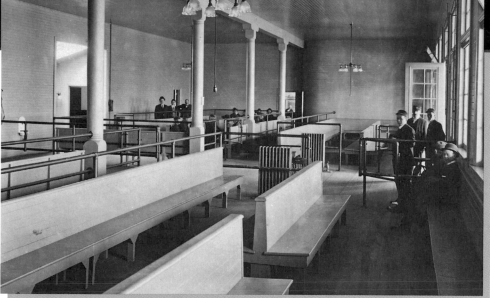

Immigrants were questioned about their family in Angel Island's examination room.

since they were last in China. Things change and memories fade, making a match unlikely, if not impossible.

This type of questioning usually lasted two or three days. However, immigrants might have to wait months for the results. Some immigrants were held at Angel Island for as long as three years. Those who failed to answer their questions correctly were deported. One Chinese man said people knew that "if the guard came in and called out a name and said 'sai gaai' [good luck], that meant that a person was free to [enter the United States]. If an applicant was to be deported, the guard would make motions as if he were crying."

CONDITIONS AT ANGEL ISLAND

Immigrants detained at Angel Island lived in a two-story wooden building called a barracks. It was surrounded by a barbed-wire fence to prevent them from escaping. Inside the building were two long rooms. The men slept in one room and the women slept in the other. Each room contained rows of narrow bunk beds. Two, sometimes three, people slept in the bunk beds, which were stacked

A barracks housed Chinese and Japanese immigrants detained at Angel Island.

one on top of the other. Often, 70 to 100 people lived there at one time. Usually, immigrants spent most of their day locked in the barracks while a guard stood outside.

For meals, the immigrants went to a big dining hall. There were two meals a day, and men and women ate at separate times to keep them from talking with one another. Most immigrants complained that the food was poor.

Immigrants ate their meals in the immigration station's simple dining room.

33

One person said, "All the dishes, including the melon, were all chopped up and thrown together like pig slop. … After looking at it you'd lose your appetite."

The days were long and boring. To pass the time, immigrants played games or read newspapers and books. Some just napped or washed their clothes. The women usually sewed or knitted. People could write as many letters as they wanted. However, officials read every letter going out or coming in. For entertainment, people sang or played music. Those who brought musical instruments with them from China formed a music club and played every night.

The immigrants had little opportunity to go outside. At set times, they could exercise or play ball in a small, fenced-in yard. Then once a week, accompanied by a guard, they could go to the docks where the luggage was kept. They were allowed to go through their luggage and take whatever belongings they needed.

A Christian church group tried to help the immigrants. The Women's Home Missionary Society sent

Katherine Maurer to Angel Island. Known as the "Angel of Angel Island," Maurer did a lot to make the immigrants' stay at Angel Island better. She brought toys to the children and small items such as towels and soap to the adults. She also helped the women and children write letters and learn English.

Katherine Maurer (at right) worked with Angel Island immigrants for nearly 30 years.

Living at the immigration station was a terrible experience for the immigrants. In 1922, even the U.S. commissioner general of immigration said that the buildings were dirty firetraps and not fit for humans. Unfortunately, little changed for the immigrants until a fire destroyed the main building in 1940. Then the government abandoned the station and moved the immigrants to San Francisco. The station was never used for immigrants again.

36

Immigrants detained at Angel Island helped put out a fire in the main building.

Eventually, the government gave Angel Island to the state of California for a state park.

Being locked up like criminals made most of the immigrants angry. They did not eat or sleep well. Without the comfort of their families, the immigrants felt lonely and afraid. They worried that they had risked their families' life savings to come to the United States only to be told that they could not stay. Many of them expressed how they felt in poems, such as this one, found written on a barracks wall:

Imprisoned in the wooden building day after day,
My freedom withheld; how can I bear to talk about it?
I look to see who is happy but they only sit quietly.
I am anxious and depressed and cannot fall asleep.

Over the years, many of the poems had been covered by paint. They were not considered important until 1970. Just when the buildings were going to be destroyed, park ranger Alexander Weiss discovered the poems and notified

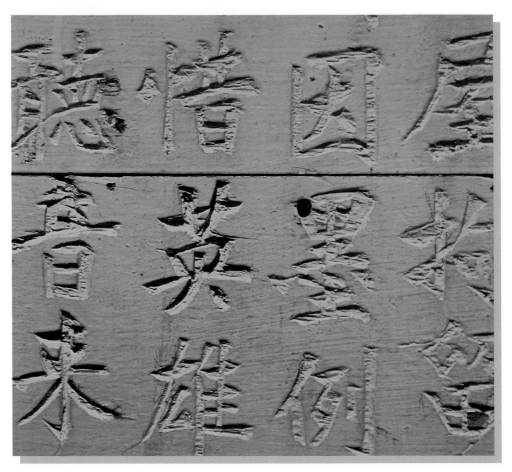

Immigrants carved poems and other writings on the walls of the barracks.

authorities. After a careful search, more than 100 poems
were found. The Chinese-American community rallied
together and raised money to save this historic landmark.
In 1976, the state of California set aside money to preserve
the barracks and the poems.

ANGEL ISLAND STATE PARK

Today, Angel Island is a state park and a National

Historic Landmark. It is a popular place for people to

visit. On a tour of the island you can see the various ways

Today, sailboats—not steamships—sail the waters around Angel Island.

39

Visitors come to Angel Island to learn about its history and enjoy its natural beauty.

the land has been used over the years. There are military
buildings from the Civil War era and government missile
sites from the 1950s. A small museum on the island tells
the story of Angel Island in words and pictures. You can
also visit the old barracks building at the immigration
station. A museum there features the men's barracks and
some of the poems that the men carved into the walls. The

40

poems remind us of the sacrifices these people made to come to the United States.

Angel Island is no longer the "Guardian of the Western Gate." As a state park, it welcomes everyone. As a National Historic Landmark, it honors the people and events that contributed so much to American history.

Today, Angel Island hosts ceremonies to welcome new U.S. citizens.

41

GLOSSARY

citizenship—the rights, privileges, and duties that come with being a citizen of a certain country

deported—sent back to one's home country

detained—held back when wanting to go

discrimination—treating people unfairly because of their race, religion, sex, or age

firetrap—a place that can easily catch on fire

immigrants—people who move from one country to live permanently in another

persecution—continually treating a person or group of people cruelly and unfairly

riot—bad behavior by a large group of people

transcontinental—crossing a continent

vineyards—land where grapes are grown

DID YOU KNOW?

- The earliest known visitors to Angel Island were Miwok Indians. For thousands of years they regularly hunted and fished there. At one time the island was also a favorite meeting place of pirates.

- In the 19th century, the Chinese emperor forbade any citizen from leaving the country. He said that he would cut off the heads of those who left and dared to return. This ruling, however, was impossible to keep and never stopped Chinese from traveling to other countries.

- Most of the Chinese who entered the United States came from the Pearl River Delta, the area around the city of Canton.

- Many of the 13,000 Chinese who worked on the transcontinental railroad went on to other railway jobs. Eventually, they were responsible for building all or part of almost every railroad line from Texas to Alaska.

- The U.S. military built a missile site on the western shore of Angel Island to protect the United States. The missiles remained there until 1962, when they were no longer needed.

IMPORTANT DATES

Timeline

1775 — Spanish explorer Don Juan Manuel Ayala gives Angel Island its name.

1848 — Angel Island becomes part of the United States.

1882 — The U.S. Congress passes the Chinese Exclusion Act to keep Chinese from entering the United States for 10 years. The law does not apply to merchants, diplomats, or students. This law continues to be renewed until the 1940s.

1910 — The Angel Island Immigration Station opens in San Francisco Bay.

1940 — Angel Island Immigration Station closes after a fire destroys one of its main buildings.

1943 — The U.S. Congress lets all Chinese enter the United States and become U.S. citizens.

1997 — Angel Island Immigration Station becomes a national historic site.

IMPORTANT PEOPLE

DON JUAN MANUEL AYALA (?–?)
Spanish explorer who named Angel Island in 1775

ANSON BURLINGAME (1820–1870)
American official responsible for the 1868 treaty between the United States and China, which gave citizens of both countries the freedom to travel back and forth from either country and stay as long as they liked

KATHERINE MAURER (1881–1962)
Woman who improved the lives of immigrants at Angel Island; sent there by the Women's Home Missionary Society, she taught English and provided towels, combs, and other necessary items

I.M. PEI (1917–)
Chinese architect who got his degree from Harvard Graduate School of Design in Massachusetts and designed such famous buildings as the John F. Kennedy Library in Boston and the entrance to the Louvre Museum in Paris

ALEXANDER WEISS (?–?)
Park ranger who discovered Chinese poems carved on the barracks walls at the Angel Island Immigration Station in 1970 and helped preserve them

WANT TO KNOW MORE?

At the Library

Brimner, Larry. *Angel Island.* Danbury, Conn.: Children's Press, 2001.

Glasscock, Sarah. *Read-Aloud Plays: Immigration.* New York: Scholastic Professional Books, 1999.

Martin, Michael. *Chinese Americans.* Philadelphia: Chelsea House, 2003.

Socnnichsen, John. *Miwoks to Missiles: A History of Angel Island.* San Francisco: Angel Island Association, 2001.

Yep, Laurence. *The Journal of Wong Ming-Chung: A Chinese Miner, California, 1852.* New York: Scholastic Press, 2000.

On the Web

For more information on the *Angel Island,* use FactHound to track down Web sites related to this book.

1. Go to *www.facthound.com*

2. Type in a search word related to this book or this book ID: 0756512611

3. Click on the *Fetch It* button.

Your trusty FactHound will fetch the best Web sites for you!

On the Road

The Immigration Station Barracks Museum
Old Barracks Building
Tiburon, CA 94920
415/435-3522
To walk through a former men's barracks and read some of the poems carved on the walls

Chinese Historical Society of America
965 Clay St.
San Francisco, CA 94108
415/391-1188
To see many items relating to the history of Chinese immigration

Look for more We the People books about this era:

The Great Chicago Fire
*Great Women of the Suffrage
    Movement*
The Harlem Renaissance
The Haymarket Square Tragedy

The Hindenburg
Industrial America
The Johnstown Flood
The Lowell Mill Girls
Roosevelt's Rough Riders

A complete list of We the People titles is available on our Web site:
www.compasspointbooks.com

INDEX

About the Author

Alice K. Flanagan writes books for children and teachers. Since she was a young girl, she has enjoyed writing. She has written more than 70 books. Some of her books include biographies of U.S. presidents and their wives, biographies of people working in our neighborhoods, phonics books for beginning readers, and informational books about birds and Native Americans. Alice K. Flanagan lives in Chicago.